What a Lucky Dog!

How To Understand
Men Through Their Dogs

What a Lucky Dog!

How To Understand
Men Through Their Dogs

Wendy Diamond
Founder & Editorial Director of Animal Fair Magazine

Animal Fair
www.animalfair.com

WHAT A LUCKY DOG!
How To Understand Men Through Their Dogs

By Wendy Diamond

Copyright © by Wendy Diamond

Published in the United States by Animal Fair Media, Inc. New York City.

For information regarding special discounts for bulk purchases, please contact Animal Fair Media, Inc. at 212 629-0392 ext 201 or luckybook@animalfair.com mailto:luckybook@animalfair.com

www.animalfair.com http://www.animalfair.com

Book design by Michelle Bada

The Library of Congress Control Number 2003098377
ISBN 0-9746691-0-5:
First Edition: February 2004

Animal Fair

To all of the dogs who have captured my heart over the years, and especially the love of my life, Lucky.

CONTENTS

INTRODUCTION

WE ALL HAVE THE PASSIONATE DESIRE to meet the ideal mate. In the United States alone there are 85 million singles looking for the right partner. My own quest for finding the perfect man lead me to discover the similarities between men and their dogs. My beautiful white Maltese, Lucky, is a dog magnet! I've met many interesting men and their various breeds of canines thanks to Lucky. As founder and editorial director of *Animal Fair*, a lifestyle magazine for animal lovers, my possibilities for meeting and dating men with different breeds of dogs through my work, travel, and adventures has been unending. So, I wanted to share my insights with curious and optimistic women around the world. *What A Lucky Dog!* is the ultimate dating guidebook for singles of all persuasions, those living or married to men with dogs, those who have a friend with a dog, or anyone searching for Mr. Right!

In Chapter 1 I will provide readers with a brief history of the canines past, present, and future. There are more than over 68 million dogs in the United States and at the end of half of those leashes are men. Dog is man's loyal best friend! Since men naturally identify with dogs, in Chapter 2 I have humorously explored finding the common link and shared personality traits between men and their dogs. Through my own amusing experiences and extensive research, I comprised a compilation of what women can expect from 32 different types of men who own certain breeds. Is an Irish Setter man always going to be at the pub? Will you be able to stay in the race with Mr. Greyhound? Are Rottweilers really dangerous? So many questions, so few answers … until now. It's common knowledge that both men and dogs have the tendency to stray. Once you find the perfect breed of man for you - how do you keep him from scratching at the front door to get out? Chapter 3 includes comical instructive training tips. Through these training tips, you'll become the master of your relationship. Although I find that every breed is different, the training tips do work, and I personally suggest you try it right from the start of your romance to promote longevity and happiness. Does your Golden Retriever man jump all over you in public? Are you tired of cleaning up Mr. Cocker Spaniel's clothes from the floor, back of the chair, or end of the bed? Is the Dober-man's over-protective barking in public getting out of control? My specific tried and true training tips will give you the skills you need to curb your man while still having great fun!

I thought what's a book about dating without success stories! In Chapter 4 I've included true circumstances where dogs have played an integral part in bringing couples together with positive results. And how dogs have altered the fates of different people and situations, probably unintentionally but constructively. The dogs in these success stories act like innocent muses, using leashes as conduits to create divine intervention and happy endings. These stories are doggone comical and real. I'm so positive that you'll be inspired by the stories, that in Chapter 5 I've provided a list of breeders and shelters where you can purchase different breeds or adopt mutts and strays.

I'm still single, dating, and looking to find the ideal man, and true love! I'm only half way through dating the breeds of men listed in my book! My dog Lucky has put the bark out for me amongst her canine crowd at the dog run, so I'm sure it won't be long until I find Mr. Right. Let this entertaining guidebook help you figure out more about the men in your life through the dog(s) he owns. I'm confident you'll get as much enjoyment dating the different breeds, using the training tips, and reading the success stories as I did writing this book. And when you do meet the perfect man, *What a Lucky Dog!*

Chapter 1

History of Dogs & Men

The greater love is a mother's; then comes a dog's; then a sweetheart's.
Polish Proverb

Have you ever wondered where the word Dog originates? It's a shortened version from the Latin term Canis (dog) familiaris (domestic). Scientists recently discovered in 1997 through new molecular genetic techniques (love that technology) that man's best friend is actually much older than first thought. Men are like dogs, identify with dogs, and share a long history with canines. Dogs can be genetically traced possibly as far back as 100,000 years or more. Originally it was believed that dogs were only 20,000 years old. The new scientific discovery confirms that dogs evolved from wolves. The Latin term Canis familiaris (dog) was changed in the 1990's to Canis lupus (wolf) familiaris. Maybe this latest scientific information explains your dog and man's wild behavior and howling on full moons!

The first recorded history of human relationships with dogs began 20,000 years ago. Prehistoric men first began to use dogs for hunting, so women really can't blame today's men for their instinct to flirt – they've got thousands of years of the game and chase behind them! It wasn't until 5,000 to 7,000 years ago that dogs were domesticated as important protectors, guards, and worked alongside humans. Various Roman and Asiatic dog bloodlines were spread with local dogs throughout Europe during different invasions and wars. Breeding and training became important for improved hunting, herding, and guarding skills.

Throughout history man's closest companion, his dog, traveled everywhere with him. Attributing to the expansion of many breeds from Europe, to the Middle East, to the United States. And you think your man gets around! Some breeds gained and lost popularity at critical times throughout civilization because of royal favoritism, the crusades and inquisition, war, famine, plagues and usefulness.

Luckily, during the 1900's various organizations were created to prevent breeds from going extinct and many shelters were established to promote finding homeless and stray dogs permanent homes (see Chapter Five for a list of organizations). We don't want to lose any of the darling breeds and mutts that have become such a cherished part of our daily lives!

Dogs have served many purposes throughout time. They were used for hunting, protecting, herding, and as quiet confidants. Many presidents, celebrities, and successful business people found solace in the unconditional love dogs provide. Earlier this century, when a man was called a "dog" it meant he was a scoundrel or cad. Presently in modern pop culture the term "dog" or "dawg" means positive social identification for a man from his inner circle or posse.

What a Lucky Dog! has taken this one step further by providing a dating guidebook for women, defining the men in their lives through the dog he owns. I foresee a new wave in pop culture emerging. A man won't be vaguely called a "dog" anymore - he'll be humorously defined and nicknamed by the breed or mutt he owns! He'll now be a "Dober-man", a "Lab man", "Mr. Beagle", "Mutt Man", and so on.

Here are some fun historic facts about dogs! The world's largest, heaviest, and longest dog was recorded in 1989. An Old English Mastiff named Zorba that weighed 343 lbs and was 8 feet 3 inches long from nose to tail! Can you imagine feeding this dog everyday? The world's smallest dog is a tiny Yorkie from Blackburn, England. Fully grown was only 2.5 inches tall, 3.75 inches long and weighed only 4 ounces. Watch where you step! The oldest recorded reliable age for a blessed dog is 29 years, 5 months for a Queensland 'heeler' named Bluey in Victoria, Australia. That's over 206 years old in human years!

Ladies, we should celebrate the scientists who proved that all the different breeds of dogs are direct descendants of the wolf. Wolves are monogamous and mate with one partner for life. The historical facts favor women desiring a blissful lifetime commitment with just one man!

DOG BREEDS & MEN

I wonder if other dogs think poodles are members of a weird religious cult.

Rita Rudner

Is it by chance a man chooses a Great Dane or Poodle as his constant companion and best friend? Or is it because they share similar personality traits and that he can specifically identify with a certain breed? We'll look at the most popular breeds to gleam insight into their male human companions. Of course, like many people, not all dogs and men are purely one breed or another, so I've included a mutt description. If you know that your man's mutt is half German Shepherd and half Collie, read both of these descriptions to get a better understanding of his more complex personality. And have fun using this chapter to try and figure out exactly what type of mutt your man is!

This is a guide for all of you who are single, dating, committed, or merely curious in figuring out if your male companion is sincerely loyal and true blue, marriage material, a pack hound, or a hopeless roamer too distracted to commit. You'll gain insight as to what you can expect from a date with a certain breed, the profession he might choose, if children are in his future, and celebrity examples to identify with.

Next, I will take you one step further and let you know what you can expect from a certain breed when he's feeling a bit naughty and mischievous. Does an Irish Setter honestly stay out all night at the pub? Is a Rotweiler's bark really worse than his bite? Can a Greyhound slow down enough to commit? Inside, you'll find essential answers and much more to help you decide if you can handle a certain breed's wilder side.

We've all heard the saying; *You can't teach an old dog new tricks*. I'm going to give you constructive hints on how to help each different breed work on certain personality weaknesses! Since certain breeds resist constructive criticism and learning new ways of behaving, this chapter gives you the necessary inside information you need to curb your man! Have fun discussing each breed with girlfriends over Sunday brunch, co-workers during lunch, your mother or sisters over dinner, or even with your special man while walking his dog to the local dog run! Here we go!

Akita

Personality
Sushi, anyone? Mr. Akita's heritage stems from the exotic land of Japan. His ancestors didn't step foot (or should I say paw) in America until 1937. This Samurai man is quiet, strong, independent, and stubborn. He's not above getting into a verbal or physical wrestling match if he thinks those he loves are in danger. He can over-react and be over-protective. Therefore, if you're a social animal, this isn't the breed for you. If you enjoy being a geisha girl in search of a devoted homebody and protective family man, look no further. The Akita man is loyal beyond belief.

The ideal first date would be a quiet dinner for two at home with a table placed with origami, tempura, a little sake to relax him, and a large bowl of good conversation. Besides being physically powerful, he's also intelligent and well mannered. Mr. Akita needs a large dose of daily physical exercise, so take off that kimono already, put on your jogging shoes, and encourage him to take a run through the park with you. The perfect profession for this man is banker, international business executive, recording studio owner, restaurant owner or jazz musician. For example, *Saturday Night Live* legend and *Blues Brother*, Dan Akroyd, is an Akita man who loves to howl the blues and jazz. Evander Holyfield channeled his Akita samurai fighting energy to boxing. Elvis Stojko is an ice-skating Akita Olympian. Akita men feel especially feisty in cooler temperatures. Your winter months will be active, warm, and stimulating. This man will make you feel loved no matter what season it is!

Naughty Dog
The Akita man can be very domineering. His constant need to guard and protect can make him think his way is the only way, for the good of all. He's leery of new people, which can make it difficult for a newcomer to enter the clan.

A New Trick
Tell Mr. Akita to, *Lighten up*! He can be very standoffish when meeting people or in social situations. He doesn't trust anyone besides his inner circle. Slowly get him use to the idea that everyone isn't his enemy. By example, you can show him that it's safe to let his guard down every now and then!

Basset Hound

Personality

Do you remember the affectionate cartoon character Pepe Lepew? He was the lovable French skunk, and once he caught the scent of a woman, pursued her to the ends of the earth proclaiming undying love. Mr. Basset Hound's personality is very similar! He'll sniff you out with a deliberate and focused pursuit. In other words - he'll be hot on your trail! After Mr. Basset Hound has tracked you down, you'll find he's a well-mannered, soulful, and sensitive man with a playful nature. His quirky and goofy mannerisms can keep you chuckling to yourself all day long.

One of his favorite activities is trail hiking. The Basset Hound man takes pride in his reputation for being a talented hiker. Here's the catch, he becomes so involved in following one trail to its end that he gets easily sidetracked and lost without looking at other possible trails. Head for the hills with him and study the trail map before leaving. Give him subtle directions and options without him realizing it. This approach also applies for any road trips you decide to take with Mr. Basset Hound. Your target destination might be Boston, but pack your swimsuit because you might end up in Miami!

The Basset Hound's desired occupation might be a travel agent, rock climber, architect, highway designer, and engineer, door-to-door salesman or postman. *Dirty Harry* Basset Hound, Clint Eastwood hikes the trails of Carmel. Don't get discouraged if navigating your highway to love with the Basset Hound man becomes a maze of winding twists, turns, detours, and roadblocks. Take heart! He's well worth the hassle. Keep your eye on the ultimate destination point - the altar!

Naughty Dog

The Basset Hound man will treat your possessions as if they belong to him. Unintentionally, he can be destructive with others' belongings. He'll break your favorite toys without meaning to. And when you try to discuss the situation, he'll get defensive and stubborn. Making it even more difficult to reclaim your territory!

New Trick

The Basset Hound man needs regular daily exercise. He tends to move slowly and he has a weak back that requires strengthening. Explain to him that preventative medicine is the best policy, and will thwart worse back problems when he's an older hound.

Beagle

Personality

Watch out, he's a heartbreaker Ladies! The Beagle man possesses the lethal combination of being handsome and sensitive. He's a fox-hound! You'll be mesmerized with him at the first hello. Don't be fooled by his sweet shy nature because he's quite courageous, has the stamina of ten Huskies, and he knows who's boss. Didn't you know? He's the boss or at least he thinks so (wink-wink).

Mr. Beagle is a social creature and loves being one of the guys. If he wants to hang out with his buddies on the weekends, don't feel left out or neglected. Instead suggest that you and your girlfriends meet up with him and his posse, at a happening nightclub, or your local park for a Sunday afternoon game of football or baseball. He's very high strung and any physical activity the two of you can do together in and out of the bedroom - all the better for your relationship. Mr. Beagle will have a career as an ambulance driver, chef, train conductor, fireman, or professor. Howling Beagle man, Barry Manilow croons about finding romance at the *Copa Cabana* and sings endless love songs. The Beagle man has the inherent potential to be perfect marriage material. He wants children and thrives in a steady home life. Breakfast, lunch, and dinner are sacred times of day for the Beagle man. Get your culinary skills in tip-top shape because this man can eat, and eat, and....

Naughty Dog

Mr. Beagle loves to yap, bark, and vocalize. Don't be surprised when you go to powder your nose at dinner, and return to your seat, to find Mr. Beagle engaged in an endless conversation with the stranger sitting at the next table. It's wonderful that he's so outgoing, but his constant chattering might get exhausting. Once you gain his full attention back at dinner, he'll charm his way right over to your plate and take a big bite of whatever he desires.

A New Trick

You're going to have to be tolerant when housebreaking this pup! Mr. Beagle is stubborn and slow to change. If you charm him with fun and laughter, before you know it you'll have him eating out of the palm of your hand, not off your plate.

Bernese Mountain Dog

Personality

If country living is the life for you than so is the Bernese Mountain Man! He's a calm, loyal, and sensitive man who loves the great outdoors. Mr. Bernese Mountain man is very muscular, strong, likes daily exercise, and manual labor. He doesn't survive very well in urban and city apartment dwellings - too many people make him nervous. So does hot weather, he excels in cooler climates. He'll perpetually choose open pastures to crowded restaurants and cafes. His ancestors lived in the Swiss Alps and the open air gets his juices flowing.

This man has a built-in people phobia and will spend all of his time exclusively with his girlfriend, wife, and family. Strangers are non-gratis as far as he's concerned! He's wonderful father material and a protective provider. If you're a high-powered career woman with a healthy income, and desire to have children without quitting your job, Mr. Bernese Moutain Man is the perfect stay at home dad! No stuffy offices or boardrooms for this man! Instead the Bernese Mountain Man prefers a profession as a farmer, agriculturist, landscaper, consultant with a home office, writer, producer, horticulturist, or soccer coach. Passionate Bernese Mountain Man Robert De Niro has starred in the movies *Wag the Dog, Mad Dog & Glory*, and *Deer Hunter*. He frequently escapes the city to his widespread mountain ranch. If you desire birds chirping in the morning instead of horns honking, fresh air instead of smog, or you don't mind commuting everyday from the country to the city, then share the peaks and valleys of life with the Bernese Mountain Man!

Naughty Dog

You can't leave the Bernese Mountain Man alone for one second. He suffers from severe separation anxiety and can become very rebellious when he thinks he's being deserted, even to the point of throwing a tantrum and messing up the house as a cry for more attention!

New Trick

Teach the Bernese Mountain Man to socialize, get over his people phobia, and allow for new different characters to join his inner kingdom. Otherwise the country air might get a bit too retiring, stifling, and claustrophobic for you!

Bichon Frise

Personality

Camera, lights, action! It's show time as soon as you meet the Bichon Frise man. His curious, playful, cute, and talkative demeanor will captivate you when you first meet him. This man is the artistic actor, brilliant producer, witty comic, or creative dancer who craves center stage. Performing and directing is in his blood and a natural for him. The Bichon Frise ancestors spent centuries as street performers throughout Europe and especially in France.

He's a friendly fellow, ready to entertain you, your friends, or a complete stranger at the drop of a hat. You can take him to any cultural event from Broadway to the local playhouse. His eyes will light up when he feels inspired and discovers new material to enhance his own repertoire. The only problem might be if the Bichon Frise man gets too much in the moment - he might spontaneously jump up on stage uninvited and embarrass you. Successful Hollywood Bichon Frise men in the entertainment industry are Martin Scorcese and Aaron Spelling.

If you find this man matches your Juliet with his Romeo, and the two of you create the perfect love story (no matter how satirical) - he's all yours! Mr. Bichon Frise is great with children, and he's the kind of dad who won't mind dressing up as a clown on birthdays, or Santa on Christmas. And you'll live happily entertained forever after....

Naughty Dog

The Bichon Frise man's constant need to be in the limelight can be unnerving. His super ego might need to be checked in at the coat check every now and again. It might behoove him to let others have their fifteen minutes of fame in the spotlight!

New Trick

Yes, he's a dreamer and living in the real world of responsibility might not be his strong suit. It's up to you to teach Mr. Bichon Frise that money is important to survive and can allow him a certain amount of creative freedom. If you have friends in the biz, introduce him to the art of networking.

Boston Terrier

Personality

Made in the U.S.A.! Mr. Boston Terrier is a dapper home grown whose ancestors trace back to the early English settlers. He's an outgoing, extremely energetic Blue Blood. The Boston Terrier man is an interesting mix of rugged American brawn and sweet gentlemen. When you first meet him he will show his receptive well-mannered side. Mr. Boston Terrier will be attentive and caring on your first romantic dinner date together. It's the party afterwards that you should be concerned about! In a New York minute the Boston Terrier man can switch from Mr. Savoir Faire to Mr. Rock n' Roll party boy (no matter what his age). He possesses a wild side and loves to play all types of games, on and off the court. You're barking up the wrong tree if you can't keep up with the Boston Terrier man's quick paced lifestyle. He loves the city life!

His professional calling will find him in the position of entertainment producer, promoter, designer, restaurant entrepreneur, pilot, politician, real estate developer or any occupation where he can utilize all facets of his personality. All-American Terrier President Teddy Roosevelt was an avid hunter, raised six children, and federally protected over 230 million acres of U.S. soil! He was also the inspiration for the endearing term, "teddy bear"! These sensitive men rock climb, ride motorcycles, fly planes, and take chances while still finding the time to adore and pamper the women in their lives. Life with the Boston Terrier man guarantees to be a Boston tea party!

Naughty Dog

If the Boston Terrier man sets his sights on you and you become the focus of his heart's desire - watch out! You might have to buy a watchdog to monitor his strong prey-drive. All the attention might be flattering, but there's a fine line between being pursued and being consumed. Sometimes Mr. Boston Terrier crosses the line and needs to be firmly told: "Stay"!

New Trick

The Boston Terrier man has an innate tendency to become distracted when his party playful side emerges. Three keywords that will help you center this man are patience, consistency, and praise. Demands don't work with him, but lots and lots of treats do!

Boxer

Personality

Do you know how to weave and bob like a prizefighter? You'll have to be in top form to stay in the ring with Mr. Boxer. The Boxer is a high-energy man with a great deal of strength and stamina. You'll notice him immediately when he enters the room. The Boxer man will amusingly approach his friends as if he's playfully going to box with them.

He's sporty and thrives on having an entertaining time whenever he can. Mr. Boxer's joy of the good life can lead him to easy distraction and trouble if he isn't disciplined. He'll amusingly try to get your goat when you first start dating him. Don't let him get to you and play along! The Boxer man is actually very sweet and sensitive after he gets to know a woman. And you won't be able to resist his cute little nose when he puts on the charm! Plan on having a large family if you start to hear wedding bells with Mr. Boxer. He's a demonstrative family man who adores children. Mr. Boxer expects to have a busy family life. If you marry this man your weeks will consist of soccer games, flea markets, barbeques, movies, weekend trips, shopping, and many rounds of scrabble and monopoly. The Boxer man will want you to keep up and share the lead! You'll have to make sure he takes breaks within his eventful schedule otherwise he'll get overheated. *Rocky's* Sylvester Stallone is a Boxer man who couldn't be kept down! Legendary *Casablanca* Boxer man Humphrey Bogart was known as a tough guy with a big heart. The Boxer man might choose a career as a weight trainer, sports coach or agent, comedian, restaurant or club owner, athlete, entertainer, or deejay. He's a real knockout!

Naughty Dog

Mr. Boxer can tease you in front of his friends while getting a big kick out of it. You might feel frustrated and publicly embarrassed at the same time. Don't take it all too seriously!

New Trick

The Boxer man has to know you're in charge for him to respect and love you. You'll have to give him constant positive praise and lavish attention for him to react obediently. He secretly desires you to train him and keep him in line.

Bulldog

Personality

Ladies, step right up - introducing in the Mr. Right corner, *Bulldog*! Bulldog men come form a long lineage of British prizefighters. He's much more tame than his ancestors, even to the point of being good-natured. Mr. Bulldog isn't the most handsome man on the block but that won't matter once he cracks one of his famous jokes with his natural goofy style. If humor turns you on, he's the man! He's one of the most down to earth guys you're going to meet. No pretensions here! If you are a stickler for good etiquette and social graces, this isn't the man for you. Mr. Bulldog devours his food, disregarding all manners, so beware until he's trained. Think, *five-star restaurant - no; all-night diner - yes*.

Mr. Bulldog tends to be attracted to the martial arts, military, nightclub management, food caterering, or athletic coaching. Adam Sandler incorporates humor to most of his movies, such as *The Wedding Singer* and *Big Daddy*. Fred Durst of Limp Bizkit is the earthy Rock N' Rolling Bulldog man. And Jason Priestly is the racy Bulldog type.

You're going to need earplugs if you decide to spend the night, live with, or marry a Bulldog man. Yes, this guy snores and sniffles while sleeping. When you wake up in the morning snappy and barking from yet another restless night, he'll do something silly, tell a joke, and make you laugh until you forget why you are upset in the first place. It's a part of Mr. Bulldog's undeniable charm.

Naughty Dog

Mr. Bulldog can become mouthy and snappy when he feels his territory is being threatened. He just can't control his macho response. His temperament originates genetically from a long lineage of ancestral warriors and fighters.

New Trick

The Bulldog man tends to be immature and reactionary in his responses, but you can help him by gently pulling him aside and calmly explaining why such behavior at his age really isn't amusing or appropriate. Also, if you're planning to have a dinner party, offer him a much needed class in Table Manners 101. If he goes along with the lesson, meet him halfway and promise a future food fight as his reward.

Chihuahua

Personality

Chicas, say *Hola!* to the land of the Chihuahua! This Latin lover's ancestry originates from Mexico and Central America, and can be traced all the way back to the Aztec civilization. The modern Chihuahua man can be very high strung and nervous, especially in new social settings. It's important from the start that you introduce him to your close network of friends and family. Once he feels comfortable and warms up, he will delight everyone with entertaining and intellectual conversation. Mr. Chihuahua loves to be the center of attention. Don't let his small frame fool you; he's true to his Latino nature, strong and passionate.

A healthy outlet for his daily fire is a profession as a singer, dance instructor, publicist, radio personality, restaurant owner, news correspondent or construction worker. Zealous and impassioned actor Mickey Rourke is a Chihuahua man! His movies *9-1/2 Weeks* and *Angel Heart* display his ardent depth. Funny Chihuahua man George Lopez's sitcom makes light of his heritage!

Do I have to tell you what the perfect first date with a Chihuahua man should be? That's right, put on the low cut tight red dress, off for a paella and sangria dinner, and cap the night with salsa dancing at a Latin dance club. He'll beam with pride as he sashays you center stage and claims the dance floor as his rightful territory. He'll become aggressive if another man tries to cut in on his turf. Save yourself the trouble and let him know he's the only man in the room for you. The Chihuahua will feel ten feet tall!

Naughty Dog

The Chihuahua man can be very demanding and selfish if he doesn't get his own way. He possesses the nasty habit of sleeping anywhere in your apartment or house he chooses. Including snoozing on your favorite antique sofa that took you two years to find!

New Trick

It will be in your best interest not to baby the Chihuahua man. His tendency is to become verbally aggressive when he thinks he's not getting enough attention. If you have to spend days away, distract him by renting Antonio Banderas movies, leave him Carlos Santana CDs and several boxes of frozen Mexican food.

Chinese Crested

Personality

Two heads are better than one? Meet the Chinese Crested twins: Powderpuff and Hairless! As with most twins, these two men share common personality traits, yet are very different. Both Chinese Crested brothers have an alert intense expression, and a highly playful and affectionate attitude towards life! Do you want to be nurtured or nurture? Answering this question will help you choose which twin is for you. Ladies, here's the difference between these two men (it's fun to have choices). Powderpuff is the stronger, virile, outgoing, outdoorsy type, and prefers dining out and dancing all night to staying home. Hairless is the domestic indoor man because of his sun sensitive skin and weak constitution. He has to wear sun block in the summer, an extra sweater in the winter, prefers home cooked meals, and moonlit walks.

More attributes that the Chinese Crested twins share; both are friendly devoted family men and treat friends and strangers like extended family members. For this reason they make great therapists, arbitrators, party planners and fundraisers. Professions where they can bring people together. They're gifted climbers and jumpers, like the very agile Raymond twins (Neil and Adrian) from *The Matrix Reloaded*.

No matter which twin you choose, the other twin will always be in your life as a close family member. Ready, your starring in your very own reality show, drum rolls please, which one will it be: Powderpuff or Hairless?

Naughty Dog

The Chinese Crested men can be too friendly for their own good and lack discretion when bringing home strangers. You might have to get use to every Tom, Dick, and Hairy (Harry) invited to your home and social events.

New Trick

Chinese Crested men are not the greatest protectors and judges of character. They naively think all breeds are simpatico. You might want to parlay some of your woman's intuition his way. He'll thank you when the other guy gets duped or conned instead of him.

Chow Chow

Personality

Knick Knack, paddy whack, give the Chow a bone! The Chow Chow man's Chinese ancestors gave him his name, which translates to "knick knack". When you first meet the Chow Chow man you might think you've made a negative first impression because of the scowl on his face. Don't take it personally. He's just a very serious man with a reserved expression. Mr. Chow Chow treasures his independence and prefers the women he dates to keep him on a long leash. He'll snap at you if he thinks he's not free to roam when he wants. Give him some space; this man isn't a cheater. He's truly loyal and protective when in a committed relationship. And whatever you do, never sneak up on the Chow Chow man from behind or beside him. He has poor eyesight and will get jumpy and startled. Try to approach him head-on at all times!

Probing thinker and psychologist Sigmund Freud was a Chow man. Walt Disney was quite inventive when he created his animated dynasty. Actor Ethan Hawke is a Chow Chow man who chooses thought-provoking movie roles to reflect his talent.

Mr. Chow Chow can live in the city or country as long as the temperatures are cool and the space is large. Say *Ciao* (Chow!), if you're a woman who wants to have children. Most Chow Chow men aren't especially playful or good with children. But, if you're a professional woman who's decided against having children and opted for creating business ideas instead, he's the man! He'll choose a career as a farmer, cattle rancher, courier, security guard, waiter, mover, salesman or postman. The Chow Chow man is skeptical of strangers and will always shield you from suspicious types with one stern look!

Naughty Dog

Never remove the Chow Chow man's meal from the table until he's completely finished. This man gets totally engrossed when he chows down. He'll get very irritable and might bite your hand off if his food is taken away or he doesn't get enough to eat. Please warn your waiter in advance when dining out!

New Trick

You'll have to teach the Chow Chow man that he can relax with you. He's shy and doesn't like to be touched at first. Give him a massage and encourage him to let his guard down. Once he emotionally trusts you, he'll become more physically responsive.

Cocker Spaniel

Personality

Your Cocker Spaniel man likes to hang out with the crowd, but takes a more unobtrusive stance. He's the kind of guy who will go out with his buddies and remain subtly in the background. Don't let him fool you; he's still an alert hunter at heart.

This sweet, huggable, cute man is active and high-strung. He's very sociable and befriends strangers. Don't expect him to become your guard dog. Mr. Cocker Spaniel can make you feel like you're the only woman in the room, while simultaneously checking out other female cats without you noticing. He just can't stop his mischievous curiosity and will be distracted at times. Mr. Cocker Spaniel will get snappy when you call him on his behavior. He responds more positively to intelligent conversation than accusations. If you're a possessive woman in constant need of attention this isn't the man for you. But, if you're a confident woman who doesn't mind Mr. Cocker Spaniel's occasional flirting and inquisitiveness - then call this man home! Gently pull on his leash and lead him. He'll also respond positively to a teasing game of fetch. Once you do catch this man you'll joyfully discover he's great with children.

The Cocker Spaniel man excels as a fashion designer, stylist, movie director, producer, entertainment agent, court judge or actor. Cocker Spaniel man, actor Tom Selleck, prefers to be acting in front of the camera!

Naughty Dog

He's too high strung and distracted to clean up after himself. Yes, he's messy. You'll find dishes in the sink and dirty clothes in the corner. Out of the two of you, hopefully you don't mind being the more domestic one.

New Trick

To get the Cocker Spaniel man to bend to your desires, train him gently and calmly. He doesn't react well to abrupt demands or ultimatums. He's easily distracted and will escape by getting lost down a brand new unmarked trail.

Collie

Personality

Lassie - come home! The Collie man is a great friend and companion to almost everyone he meets. He's friendly and very sociable, opening his world to every stranger on the corner, pizza deliveryman, mailman, and bank teller. He might even roam off with someone he met two minutes ago if he's in one of his restless moods!

The Collie man doesn't like to be left alone for very long. You should address his constant feelings of abandonment if you don't want him to run off with a more sensitive gal. You might send him daily emails, make recurring phone calls, and mail sweet greeting cards on a regular basis, to help quell his insecurity. He has an insatiable desire to please, let him know you love the way he pleases and appreciate his efforts. Mr. Collie prefers large living spaces and does his best if he has a big backyard, even in Gotham city.

This man has enormous marriage and father potential, although he tends to group his children and treat them as one large pack, not individuals. Collie man, Matthew Broderick plays many different acting roles, recently including proud father to a new pup.

Mr. Collie is such a congenial fellow, a profession as a missionary, diplomat, school counselor, performer, talk show host, translator, negotiator, or politician, is perfect for him. If you're the type of woman who enjoys socializing and meeting new people, then Mr. Collie can lead the welcome wagon to a blissful life of picnics, soirees, parties, black tie, and social events.

Naughty Dog

Mr. Collie can disappear in a flash! Smooth Collie men are related to his Greyhound cousin, so they can be very *very* fast, dart off, and get lost without a moment's notice. His restlessness can get the best of him and roaming aimlessly might become a hobby for this sweet man.

New Trick

You might want to teach Mr. Collie that everyone he meets isn't a potential best friend and you wouldn't mind a little protection every now and then. Encourage him to enroll in a martial arts class or daily workouts, it will help him harness his extra restless energy.

Dachshund

Personality

Have you heard the saying; *Good things come in small packages?* That's what you can expect from Mr. Dachshund! He's the cute small-framed man with the curious, playful look on his face. He's always waiting for a new adventure to take him away. Hopefully, you're the experience he's searching for! Don't let Mr. Dachshund's diminutive stature fool you; he's still a hunter at heart that loves a good challenge. If you combine this trait with his comedic, trickster side, you'll find a small bundle of fun surprises. The Dachshund man thrives in the countryside and city life simultaneously. Talk to all the different sides of this man (and he does like to talk) by suggesting that you take a trip to Lake Tahoe for skiing and a comedy show. Next, plan to fly to San Francisco for a day of bargain hunting, and a night of dancing and romancing.

Dachshund is a family man too! He participates in all family activities and gets along great with children. Once you settle down with him you'll notice he practices a strange habit - he gets a kick out of digging! He won't mind weeding, planting trees and landscaping your whole yard or maybe even the entire neighborhood! He makes a highly competent construction worker, landscaper, plumber, gardener, cable or energy technician. Dachshund hockey star Wayne Gretsky dug his skates into ice for years! *Sopranos* Steve Schrippo is a Dachshund man constantly burrowing his way out of trouble on the hit show. It's as if the Dachshund man is digging to discover buried treasures. You might just be the priceless jewel he's searching for!

Naughty Dog

What's the hullabaloo about? Mr. Dachshund can be a yapper and at times vocally snappish when he feels insecure. The Dachshund man isn't above raising his voice and speaking over you when in a heated discussion. Ladies, just remember his bark is much worse than his bite.

New Trick

When the Dachshund man gets in a mood, he can become anti-social and removed. He'll spend hours alone in his den, almost to the point of becoming a recluse. You need to teach him that everyone does need down time but not to the point of going underground!

Doberman Pinscher

Personality

Your Dober-man is great marriage material. He loves having a sense of family, is a fine companion and good with children. This man gets a bad rap because of his well-known snappy temper. Hey Ladies, it stems from being possessive and protective of those he loves. What woman doesn't want to feel loved and have a strong shoulder to lean on now and again! Mr. Doberman's shielding arms create a safe haven to go home to after wrestling with the day-to-day jungle. You can curb a Pinscher (or should we say pincher) of his over-possessiveness by making him feel secure and a part of your social scene right from the start. He's very athletic and joining a gym together would be a great way to channel all his extra high energy and a healthy way to bond with him. He's loyal, trustworthy and affectionate when he feels safely placed in your life. If a Dober-man has the slightest suspicion of your friends or other males in your surrounding territory he will show his macho temper immediately and become anti-social as a show of protest. When out on the town with this man, don't play games or try to make him jealous - you might cause an embarrassing social situation.

Mr. Doberman makes an expert security specialist, fitness trainer, police officer, military man, private investigator, or homeland security agent. Celebrity trainer Doberman Radu, guards his famous clientele's health and fitness! Actor Ashley Hamilton is a handsome cavalier Doberman.

Naughty Dog

You have to make it clear right from the start that you will not put up with the Pinscher's notorious sarcasm and mouthy comments when he feels threatened. His territorial personality will make him become confrontational when he thinks another man might claim what is obviously and rightfully his. Tell him to muzzle it.

New Trick

You need to encourage Mr. Dober-man's need for security at the beginning of your relationship. Try to balance quiet evenings at home and nights out on the town. When going to a party or a family gathering immediately make him feel comfortable and part of the festivities. His friendly side will quickly surface. His bark is bigger than his bite!

Golden Retriever

Personality

Who's that soulful, sensitive, golden man sitting still in the corner? Welcome Mr. Golden Retriever into your life! Don't be hoodwinked by his low-key demeanor, he's a smooth operator. Once he spots and finds you attractive, he will instantly approach and introduce himself. This man was born to hunt and retrieve! When the games begin, so does the fun! He's playful, spontaneous and enthusiastic. Mr. Golden Retriever loves everything and everyone, including children, people and other breeds.

He's an avid swimmer and will reside by the water. He'll enjoy work as a lifeguard, coast guard patroller, resort manager, bartender, scuba diving instructor or swimming coach. Many famous Golden Retriever men that live by water and splash in the pools of success are Matt Lauer, Dave Price, Conan O'Brien, Steve Guttenberg, Enrique Iglesias, Ricky Martin and Phil Donahue. The perfect romantic first date with Mr. Retriever is dinner at a restaurant overlooking water, followed by a sizzling night of dancing at a happening club.

If you're not sure about making a commitment with the Golden Retriever man, it's better to take this relationship slowly! The word "No" isn't in his vocabulary. The Golden Retriever man will use his lovable qualities to get what he wants, when he wants it, and how he wants it. When he looks at you with those playful eyes, don't melt into submission! Otherwise, you'll have one adorable but spoiled puppy on your hands!

Naughty Dog

What's yours is his! Golden Retriever is not above going through your closets and personal belongings when you're not aware. He feels entitled to your possessions. He won't think twice about wearing your sweaters, jeans or jackets - hopefully not your dresses and pumps!

New Trick

Help Mr. Golden Retriever channel his high energy by giving him projects to do around the house or yard. When you suggest that he becomes your handyman, do so with a healthy dose of compassion. He can become subservient if he thinks you're being too harsh with him. And there's nothing sadder than seeing this man walk away with his tail between his legs.

Great Dane

Personality

Who's that godly creature that just walked into the room? Enter, Mr. *Great* Dane. Yes, he's heads above the rest. His majestic presence and kingly gait makes him impossible to miss. Don't let this gentle giant intimidate you. He's a sensitive and easygoing man. Mr. Deutsche Dogge (his background is German) is aware of his immense size and never uses his strength to wield his power over lesser mortals. He'll only unleash his enormous strength when pitted against the most formidable foe. The Great Dane man doesn't mind being noticed because he's social and friendly by nature. You can take him almost anywhere but I do suggest you avoid small crowded bars or rooms. He needs lots of legroom and just won't feel comfortable if cramped!

When buying Mr. Great Dane a birthday or holiday sweater, remember that he's a very large man. Hmmm, makes you wonder, doesn't it Ladies? The perfect profession for this man is a basketball player, public speaker, military man, politician, long distance runner, engineer, or mechanic. *Ace Ventura*, Great Dane Jim Carrey, plays a hilarious slapstick pet detective!

Mr. Great Dane is a well-mannered gentlemen and a fine companion. He's marriage material and is *Great* with children. This man is just a big softy at heart.

Naughty Dog

If you don't have a very large apartment or home, Mr. Big might become a liability. When he arrives to the party you're having with the live rock band, set aside a special section for him on the dance floor. Otherwise he might try to impress you with some creative moves, end up destroying some of your prize possessions, and accidentally knocking out your best friend instead.

New Trick

It's important that Mr. Great Dane spends an equal amount of time indoors and outdoors. You can help him balance out his enormous strength by scheduling long romantic moonlit walks, and then lead him back to your hopefully sizeable humble abode.

Greyhound

Personality

Fast, faster, fastest! This man is built for speed. Have you signed up for aerobic classes, yet? If you want to keep up with the Greyhound man you better make sure your cardiovascular is in tiptop shape. He's use to hanging with the jet set and his ancestors were known for running with the aristocratic British nobility during the 1800's. Although he prefers the fast lane, this sleek long legged hunk can be reserved, quiet, and timid at times.

Mr. Greyhound is fiercely independent. If he secretly disappears suddenly, you can bet your money on one sure thing, he can be found at the racetrack. He's sporty by nature and gets a thrill from gambling on the Indianapolis 500, Kentucky Derby, Super Bowl, the World Series, and the Olympics to the local park bocci-ball tournament. The odds are in your favor if you plan to take Mr. Greyhound on a surprise jaunt to Las Vegas, Atlantic City, or if your purse allows it, enchanting Monte Carlo. He loves his creature comforts. Make sure your hotel suite is fully equipped with all his favorite amenities, including that sexy evening wear you want to try out on him. Chances are if you roll the dice with this eager to please man, you'll end up a winner! Alien star Sigourney Weaver happily took a gamble with her Greyhound husband, Jim Simpson, artistic director and founder of Manhattan's Flea Theater.

Mr. Greyhound might be a professional racecar driver, jockey, horse breeder and trainer, ice speed skater, Wall Street day trader, or pilot.

Naughty Dog

Although the Greyhound likes high-speed situations and toys, he also has the reputation for being quite the couch potato. One minute he's superman, moving faster than then a speeding bullet ... and the next minute a bullet aimed at him wouldn't get him off the couch.

New Trick

The Greyhound man is a sprinter! He might not be able to go the distance as he burns-out quickly. You must teach him to steady his energy and educate him on endurance. Stamina is important, isn't it Ladies?

Irish Setter

Personality

Oh Danny Boy! Mr. Irish Setter is the good-looking Irish man with rich chestnut red hair. He's the strong, sturdy, and elegant man hanging out with his social pack. He has an enormous amount of energy and when he's out with his friends it's like a modern day version of *Gangs of New York*! His motto is: *The more the merrier!* He's extremely good-natured and enthusiastic when he finds something or someone he wants to hunt. Pray that you're his prey!

On your first date suggest an Irish pub that serves authentic Irish dishes such as; shepherds pie, fish and chips, beef stew. It sounds cliché, but have you ever met an Irish man who doesn't like potatoes? You're in for a social late night, with lots of laughs, singing, and carousing. He has the stamina of ten men and will perform a special jig just for you when you're home alone together.

If you get serious with Mr. Irish Setter man, you should know he's loyal, affectionate, and a family man. He'll want to have offspring but does better with small children; he doesn't have the patience for babies. The Irish Setter man is financially responsible but will choose a career that will provide a healthy outlet for all his vim and vigor. He might be a fireman, restaurant and pub owner, policeman, athlete, military man, construction worker, performer, politician, or physician.

With the Irish Setter man, you have not only found a pot of gold at the end of the rainbow, but also a heart of gold. When asked what dog encapsulates the characteristics of his ideal woman; *Saved By The Bell* and *The Other Half* costar Mario Lopez said, "The Irish Setter. They are sleek with shiny red hair. I have a thing for redheads!"

Naughty Dog

When this breed is naughty - he's very naughty! Mr. Irish Setter can party all night with his buddies and not think twice about the time, or you! So don't expect him to call you exactly when the clock strikes twelve. He gets a kick out of running with the wolves!

New Trick

Subtly explain to Mr. Irish Setter that if he wants to have those namesake pups he's already bragging about, he's going to have to settle down a bit. Help him realize that the four-leafed clover he's searching for can be found in your garden, not the pub!

Labrador Retriever

Personality

Who's the tanned Adonis in his speedo, walking on the beach, and playing Frisbee? Say hello to the Labrador Retriever man. He's an energetic, active and social man who loves the good life! If he's the object of your desire, get to the gym, and don't forget your bikini waxing! You're going to be spending most of your time at the beach. The Lab man will either live or work by the water. Plan an evening by making reservations on a private boat for dinner. Later, take a romantic dip in a moonlit ocean, swimming pool, or jacuzzi. You're sure to make a big splash with him! The Labrador Retriever man finds success as a politician, actor, athlete, entrepreneur, architect, or interior designer, with an office that overlooks water.

Former Lab President Bill Clinton often eats at the *Black Dog* restaurant while vacationing on Martha's Vineyard. Lab Rocker Keith Richards was instrumental in writing the Rolling Stones hit song, *Beast of Burden*. Actor Lab man Rupert Everett played a major role in instigating his *Best Friend's Wedding*.

You should know that Lab men have duck fetishes. He can identify with ducks because of a mutual love of water. You'll find an interior duck motif throughout his home. The perfect gag gift for him, of course, a rubber ducky for his bathtub!

The Lab man thrives when praised and appreciated. The more you give, the more you'll get with this man! Lucky you, he likes to please. Don't worry - if you hook up with Mr. Lab Retriever you won't get water logged. He welcomes a calm home life on land, grounded with children and other animals, too!

Naughty Dog

The Lab man can be mischievous, stray, and find trouble if he gets bored. It's up to you to keep him mentally stimulated and interested. If you succeed, you'll be the singular female body of water he dives in to. Splish-splash!

New Trick

Mr. Labrador Retriever spends lots of his free time at the beach and often forgets to wear sun block. It's imperative that you stress the importance of skin protection and the damage that the sun's rays can do to his sensitive skin. He'll thank you twenty years from now.

Maltese

Personality

Mr. Maltese is the guy who gets away with everything! Why? Because he can! His regal disposition and downright good looks allow him to charm his way in or out of any situation he chooses. The Maltese man can mingle with the upper echelons of society without question. He's been known to have lunch with construction workers and dinner with kings.

If your version of Mr. Right is a man who is capable of being your best friend and companion, look no further. He can proudly walk you, arm-in-arm, down any red carpet social event. Once the party begins, you'll be surprised at how he's on a first name basis with most of the guests. Prince Maltese possesses such a lovable and playful disposition that everyone rallies to his side for a good time. His highness thrives on all the extra attention! He'll verbally let you know when he feels unappreciated! And he's great with children, because he's so childlike!

Stylist extraordinaire and Maltese man, Steve Cojacaru of NBC's *Today*, is viewed by thousands of loyal fans weekly. Maltese Guitarist Richie Sambora of Bon Jovi, dated Cher and many other leading ladies before settling down with Heather Locklear. The perfect profession for Mr. Maltese is an antique dealer, party planner, real estate mogul, movie producer, painter, art collector, or dealer.

So Ladies, if you like to hold court, be seen in all the right places, and socialize till the wee hours of dawn, Maltese man is the right pooch for you.

Naughty Dog

He's the prince of his domain and feels entitled to do whatever he wants. The Maltese man is popular and spoiled by his family and friends. This can cause him to become undisciplined and difficult to live with, or date, because he doesn't keep to a schedule very well.

New Trick

Do yourself a favor and don't indulge every one of Mr. Maltese's whims. It's important to lay down the law, set boundaries, and time limitations from the beginning of your relationship. Otherwise it might become a free for all. Stop the yapping and fur from flying before it starts!

Mutt

Personality

The Mutt man is a worldly Renaissance man! He's a smart smooth operator, a lovable homebody, and athlete with a curious mind, individually or all wrapped up in one body. His background is a potpourri of different nationalities and genetic influences. You might think you're dating Mr. Labrador Retriever and suddenly while you're at the beach swimming, he becomes Mr. Greyhound and wants to dry off and head for the horse races to place a bet on a sure thing. Or, just when you're sitting down to have dinner and engage in stimulating conversation with Mr. Poodle, he does an about face and starts singing show tunes with the piano player. Yes, he's part Bichon Frise! You're going to have to remain agile, flexible, and spontaneous to keep up with the Mutt man's changing moods. You'll never be bored with Mr. Mutt because he's always unleashing a different side of his complex makeup. He has a natural humanitarian side. He can compassionately identify with diversified groups of people from different walks of life.

Mr. Mutt will choose a career in the entertainment industry, medical fields, international exporting business, non-for-profit organizations or any profession that allows him to utilize the many facets of his personality. Famous multi-talented Mutt Men actors are sexy Brad Pitt of *Thelma & Louise*, mysterious David Duchovny of *The X-Files*, and animated Alan Cummings of *X-men 2*.

Buy a computer program that helps trace your Mutt man's family tree. Invite him over for dinner and later help him discover his roots. Maybe you'll find that your ancestors and Mr. Mutt mans' lived in the same small region of a different continent hundreds of years ago.

Naughty Dog

Mr. Mutt can feel scattered and ungrounded at times causing him to make hasty decisions without thinking about the consequences. His insecurities can affect his ability to open up and become vulnerable with you.

New Trick

Teach the Mutt man that his multifaceted background makes him interesting and exciting. Encourage him to celebrate his uniqueness and share his experience with you and the world!

Pomeranian

Personality

Abracadabra from Iceland! You've just met Mr. Pomeranian and immediately you're charmed off your feet. This man is a foxy spell weaver and you'll find yourself in a love trance after the first dance. He's not a tall man but so cocky and self-confident you won't notice. Mr. Pomeranian is a bundle of energy, thrives on being busy, and working a full day.

One warning - Beware of Man! This Houdini is intelligently alert and isn't above using tricky manipulation to get you to bow to his desires. It will be difficult to break the hold he has over you! Not that you'll want him to! So what if the Pomeranian man is a little mischievous. Bad boys can be sexy. A perfect example is Pomeranian man Ozzy Osbourne, known for his outrageous live performances and hit MTV reality show!

Don't expect long cozy nights in front of the fireplace with this man. He's playful and always ready for the next great adventure but he's not very affectionate. You might get invited to go skydiving, scuba diving, bungee jumping, skateboarding, or speed boating - you get the idea. He loves living on the edge. Obviously he would make the perfect magician, lawyer, arbitrator, traveling salesman, stockbroker, business consultant or advertising salesman; any professions where he can use his talented verbal skills and charm to prove a point or close the deal.

Ladies, we all could use a little more magic in our lives and that's what you'll find with this hypnotic man.

Naughty Dog

Now you see him - now you don't! The Pomeranian man's shenanigans can get tiresome. He can be perceived as a troublemaker. His playful antics might be totally misunderstood by others. Tell his critics it's all in fun!

New Trick

The Pomeranian man's constant need for adventure might have him bouncing off the walls of your home like a jumping bean. Housebreaking will be an ongoing labor of love. Teach him that staying home alone with you can be the ultimate trip.

Poodle

Personality

Do you have a Masters degree from Harvard or Yale? Are you well versed in many conversational subjects? You better be if you have your eye on the Poodle man. The second he walks in the room, you can't help notice this intelligent and impeccably well-dressed man. He wears designer duds and grooms from head to toe. He's the pedigree with a pedicure. If you're brave enough to approach Mr. Poodle first, he'll be impressed by your confidence. Your opening line should be a witty question. Then, prepare for clever repartee (and hopefully sparks) to fly between you. Mr. Poodle Mensa man isn't above using his high IQ to outsmart you and get his own way.

The Poodle man is an exciting date because he's not only a thinker, he's also energetic and spirited! *Titanic* Poodle man Leonardo Dicaprio is spotted jet setting all around the globe! Poodle politician Winston Churchill was renown for his brilliant speeches during World War II. The Poodle man makes an excellent professor, writer, scientist, publisher, orchestra conductor, corporate CEO or clothes designer.

When planning an outing give him a long list of options to choose from. Suggest going to the circus, opera, foreign movie, jazz club, trip to the Smithsonian, or the Caribbean! He'll enjoy toying and discussing each idea in depth with you before deciding on a final destination. You'll keep the Poodle man interested by keeping him intellectually stimulated. By the way, if he does choose the trip to the Caribbean, pack your bikini, the Poodle is a natural born swimmer.

Naughty Dog

This guy is the absentminded professor type! While you're in the middle of a stimulating conversation with him, he'll jump up and run to his computer to jot down yet another new idea. When the Poodle man finally gets around to cooking you that gourmet meal he promised, he suddenly remembers to call his business partner. Thirty minutes later his special béarnaise sauce burns and he orders a pizza instead.

New Trick

Mr. Poodle instigates intellectual contests of wills when he's bored and unfocused. If he gets involved in a disciplined competitive sport he'll become less argumentative and scattered. He responds very well to praise. Such a good Poodle man!

Pug

Personality

Give the Pug a welcome hug! Mr. Pug is the funny looking man with big bold expressive eyes. And yes, he could use some moisturizer on those laugh lines. Blame his ancestors for his wrinkles! They traveled and moved from ancient China, to Europe, and finally to the United States. Exhausting just thinking about it! Mr. Pug man is a diminutive man, but still confident, playful, and a dignified companion. By far, his most distinctive attribute is his witty sense of humor. Laughter is a well-known aphrodisiac and Mr. Pug will have you turned-on with a smile. He's a show-off and has a reputation for cavorting around town. Don't let this intimidate you, instead get dressed to the nines and join him!

Are you worried that the Pug man isn't serious enough to settle down and make a firm commitment? He is highly affectionate, likes to please, a true best friend and family man. When you do get to house hunting together, choose a city or town with cooler climates, such as Seattle or San Francisco. He doesn't do well in the heat.

The Pug man's chosen profession might be comedy writer, comedian, school or camp counselor, restaurant maitre d', teacher or personnel executive. He excels in occupations where social skills, leadership and levity are required. *Cheers* to funny sitcom Pug men Ted Danson and Woody Harrelson, for comically entertaining audiences for over two decades! Mr. Pug will have you laughing all the way to the altar.

Naughty Dog

Although Mr. Pug is a sweetie at heart, he does have a very stubborn streak. He can be quite obstinate and mouthy when opposed. Sometimes he possesses the awkward *foot-in-mouth* syndrome. The Pug man can crack a joke at exactly the wrong time.

New Trick

The Pug man is always on the go and can get so distracted that he may forget to put on his shoes before he walks out the front door. Show him that repetition and a balanced schedule will keep his life more organized.

Rottweiler

Personality

Mr. Rottweiler is a Roman gladiator at heart. Hail Caesar! His Italian roots travel back to the days of Roman troop marches on their way to victory. Today, you might find the Rottweiler man sporting a security guard uniform, secret service shades or military boots.

Rottweiler man Will Smith wore dark shades in *Men in Black* and shot it out with the bad guys in *Wild Wild West*. He's also known in Hollywood as being very protective of his wife Jada, and their children. The Rottweiler man's natural instinct is to guard any territory he feels responsible for, whether it's his country, bank account, or family. Hopefully if all goes as planned, he'll want to shelter you too! He's very confident and can make a quick decision when needed.

Mr. Rottweiler is self-assured, smart, courageous and domineering. If you'd like to find a way to bond with this man go straight for his heart. Enroll both of you in a weekend afternoon karate or fencing class. Then it's off to an epic war movie, and cap the night with a plate of pasta and bottle of vino at a cozy corner Italian restaurant. He'll be crooning your praises! When he mentions he wants to bring you home to meet Mama - make sure you go! The Rottweiler man wants to marry, have children, and carry on his family name, but not before he gets his mother's approval. He's a traditional family man and herds his relatives together whenever he can. Holidays are a special and joyous time with Mr. Rottweiler!

Naughty Dog

The Rottweiler man can be as bossy as *The Godfather*. His desire to protect can become overly compulsive and obsessive when dealing with those he loves. Highly wary of strangers, he's not above using one of his many connections to check out your long lost friend who suddenly reappears at your front door step.

New Trick

You'll need the patience of an angel when trying to quell Mr. Rotteweiler's suspicious mind. This isn't a small task and will take tolerance and perseverance on your part. Your best approach will be to introduce him to new people and social settings in recurring dates. Once he feels comfortable, he'll surprise you by keeping it loose.

Saint Bernard

Personality

Do you want to be rescued by love? Then Mr. St. Bernard is the man to find and save you. This tall, patient, and calm man might not be the life of the party but he is one of the most responsible gentlemen around. If you bark up his family tree, you'll discover that his roots started back in Switzerland, and his relatives were known for search and rescue missions throughout the region. So Swiss Miss, get your best yodel voice in shape and call this man home.

St. Bernard man is likely to be working with the coast guard, various search party groups, as a fireman, lifeguard, paramedic, private investigator, FBI agent, or any vocation where he can use his natural instinct to locate the injured and missing. Charles Grodin plays a dependable St. Bernard man in the animal-friendly *Beethoven* movies. The St. Bernard's stature might be deceiving; he looks too large to move for long periods of time. He has a great deal of stamina, is dependable in emergency situations and provides a certain level of security. This savior of a man can be your very own Rock of Gibraltar.

A fun recreational date would be to create your own seek and find drill. Take him to a mountainside, local park, crowded beach, or packed dance club. Tell him you're going for a short walk alone and if you're not back in ten minutes, he should find you. Don't return and leave clues along the way; your scarf wrapped around a tree, a message in the sand, send a waiter over with a note on a napkin, etc. While he's searching for you, sneak up behind him! Later, reward your St. Bernard man for being such a good sport with a hot cup of cocoa or something much sweeter.

Naughty Dog

The St. Bernard man isn't always a saint! He can be very stubborn and moves at his own pace. You might feel you have to hire a bulldozer to get him off the couch or floor. He won't budge when he doesn't want to. And what's with the drooling, already!

New Trick

You might feel as if you have to set off fireworks around Mr. St. Bernard to get him excited about anything that isn't a life or death situation. He's a fine solo companion; introduce him to the idea that life can be a bowl of cherries and great fun when he socializes with others more often.

Shih Tzu

Personality

Shih Tzu, (whose name translates to "lion dog"), is the original Zen Man. His ancestry originated in Tibet, and he comes from a long line of Buddhists. Ancient Chinese royalty took a special liking to his ancestors. The Shih Tzu man is the upbeat, sweet, thin, toned, wiry guy with the long beautiful mane of hair (hopefully not more luxurious than yours). Don't let his small frame fool you, he has a lot of energy and can be quite tough if situations require him to be. This man needs a healthy dose of daily exercise. Shih Tzu men might choose a career as a performer, yoga instructor, philosophy professor, hairdresser, spiritual adviser or astrologer. Legendary crooner Frank Sinatra was a Shih Tzu man. He howled and hunted with his very own *Rat Pack*! Shih Tzu boy band Hanson sang and chanted *MMMbop*, all the way to the top of the pop charts! And Shih Tzu billionaire Bill Gates created a computer worldwide change of consciousness with Microsoft.

When you start dating Mr. Shih Tzu, sign up together for a yoga class at the local center, gym, or ashram. After class it's back to your temple of love. Light some incense, dim the lights, play ethereal new age music, order Chinese take-out, and watch this man become your gentle lapdog. Hey, if you help him balance his *chi*, Shih Tzu man might propose on one knee. Yes, he's marriage material and great with children. If you do decide Mr. Shih Tzu is the one, your morning mantra should be: *Ohmmm...Shih Tzu man, commitment is at hand*.

Naughty Dog

The Shih Tzu man does have a prominent stubborn streak he hides behind his playful nature. When a point of contention arises between the two of you he might not budge an inch. Teach him the ancient art of compromise. He'll reach his much sought after nirvana sooner!

New Trick

Mr. Shih Tzu prefers to keep his lion's mane hair long. Sometimes he wears a ponytail. He might start to look like a madman or wacky professor if he doesn't groom and properly take care of his hair. The next time you go shopping for shampoo and conditioner, pick up some hair products for your Shih Tzu man, and introduce him to the world of hair care.

Siberian Husky

Personality

Mush! That's what will happen to your heart the second you meet Mr. Siberian Husky. He's the handsome Russian hunk with the gorgeous blue or brown eyes. And they don't call him *husky* for nothing! He's strong, powerful, fast, and has great endurance. The Siberian Husky man's character is a sturdy combination of clever wit, mischievous adventure, and stubborn independence.

Your dating progress with the Siberian Husky man will move along quicker if you sincerely like his closest friend. His friend is going to be a big part of the overall picture! These two fun-loving buddies practically do everything together. They can spend hours discussing a gamut of subjects from Olympic competitions, government conspiracy plots, newest styles of jeans, to their next skiing excursion. At least the conversations won't get boring!

Mr. Siberian Husky performs better in cooler temperatures and prefers to live closer to the Canadian border than south of the border. If you do settle down and have little Eskimos with this man, your winter months will be full of fun games and sports. The Siberian Husky man has a preference for outdoor professions such as a snow plower, ski instructor, military transport engineer, landscaper, construction builder, long distance runner, excavator, or sled racer. This man promises to pull you through the different terrains of commitment with effortless ease, fun adventure, and loving affection. *Zoolander* funnyman Ben Stiller is a Husky man who pulls his weight with laughter! Husky joker Tom Green goes the distance in *Road Trip*!

Naughty Dog

The late night carousing and clever capers that Mr. Siberian Husky and his best friend are always planning can get quite tiresome when you want some private time alone with this man. He's not above barking loudly when opposed!

New Trick

The trick here is to *teach* him a trick. The Siberian Husky man resists change and modifying any of his behaviors is going to take patience on your part. Offer him as many treats possible without spoiling him!

West Highland Terrier

Personality

Do you hear the faint sound of Scottish bagpipes getting closer? That's Mr. West Highland Terrier entering your life. You'll recognize him immediately! He's the guy with the great teeth and friendly smile. Don't worry about making the first move. He's curious and independent enough to approach you without hesitation. The West Highland Terrier man has the gift of gab, and makes everyone he meets feel comfortable right from the start, including you! Once the preliminaries are over, don't be surprised when he invites you to an outing. This man loves the great outdoors. Go out and buy that kayaking, mountain climbing, and bike gear if you plan on dating him seriously. The worse that can happen is you'll get in great shape and he won't mind when your tummy gets toned.

Mr. West Highland is affectionately demonstrative albeit demanding. He'll expect you to keep up with his full itinerary. He has an insatiable hunger for being in the know, and in the middle of what's happening. For this reason, he's a natural politician, news or sports reporter, commentator, actor, journalist, professor, teacher, or public relations executive.

Designer West Highland Terrier man, Tommy Hilfiger, fits this profile as his clothing designs are seen on many celebs and their dogs! If Mr. West Highland Terrier's schedule is too busy for you - then head east. But if you do, you'll miss out on answering an age-old mysterious question. Exactly what is underneath that kilt?

Naughty Dog

The West Highland Terrier man is highly sociable and doesn't like to make waves. Diplomacy is his middle name and he believes in letting bybones be bybones - whoops - bygones be bygones. Although he's very loyal, don't expect him to fight your battles for you. He prefers to keep the atmosphere light and avoids heated confrontations.

New Trick

What's the rush? Between Mr. West Highland Terrier's outdoor activities and his social calendar - when will you ever find quality time alone together? You'll have to teach him that your private time can be as exciting and fulfilling as the next grand opening. Fads fade but true love lasts!

Yorkshire Terrier

Personality

Mr. Yorkshire Terrier is that cutie in the window, the one with the waggley tail! He's the guy with that irresistible, inquisitive face, which draws you closer with each look. Don't let his small stature trick you; he's a fearless man with a propensity for trouble and adventure. Mr. Yorkie isn't above starting quarrels with anyone that opposes his opinions, and even gets a rise out of verbal sparring matches, even with a complete stranger. That's what makes him the quintessential lawyer, arbitrator, business manager, or agent. Ladies, his adorable, impeccable looks, british wit, and energized spirit convince everyone that he's the man of the hour and should be listened to. The Yorkshire Terrier man is a big man in a small body, and double for his ego! If he's charmed you, he'll let you know from the start that he's the boss, whether you're out on the town or at home. He's so lovable that you'll probably give in to his demands, hopefully for your sake within reason.

Mr. Yorkie is usually not the outdoors type and prefers indoor activities. Yorkie man quarterback Brett Favre of the Green Bay Packers is an exception. He's known for being a calculating tough player on the field and a playful big kid at heart off of it!

The average Yorkie man partakes in short bouts of exercise, but favors mental gymnastics and marathons. Expect him to have at least fifty explanations on why working out is overrated and unnecessary. Your rebuttal; tell your Terrier man you expect him to keep up when court recesses, and the two of you create a sexy, private, world class action suit at home.

Naughty Dog

The Yorkshire Terrier man does like his creature comforts and prefers to stay home on his free time. He turns the household upside down, makes a huge mess, and doesn't mind falling asleep in his dirty clutter.

New Trick

Mr. Terrier can have a slight Napoleon complex, causing him to compensate for his sleight size by talking back and being bossy. You'll have to build and soothe his sensitive ego, convincing him that he's perfect as is, and that's why you love him so!

TRAINING TIPS TO KEEP YOUR MAN

Here, Gentlemen, a dog teaches us a lesson in humanity.

Napoleon Bonaparte

"MEN ARE DOGS!" Many different women dating a gamut of breeds (and mutts) of men have howled this for many different reasons. This chapter will provide you with a guideline of specific humorous training tips and canine commands to follow if you want to be more in control of your relationship. Remember, Ladies, the first two months are critical when disciplining your man; from day one it's up to you to set the tone for the whole relationship. Don't be shy, shorten that leash, give your commands and take charge if you think this man is the one! Have you ever wanted to tell your man "No" before and didn't know how to do it without making him upset or offending him? I'll enlighten you on how and when it's the appropriate time to use this canine command and other commands such as; "Come", "Sit", " Stay", "Down", and "Roll Over". You'll enjoy trying the commands on your man and finding the correct use for each new situation when necessary. Your breed might not understand what's happening at first but before he knows it he'll be out of the doghouse and happily in your arms. That's the perfect time to bestow him with unique treats only you can supply and he finally deserves.

Housebreaking a man can be one of the most difficult tasks a woman can undertake when she decides to marry or cohabitate. I will provide an instructive training tip on how to go accomplish this task with ease and levity. Before long your man will be scratching and barking at the front door to get in - not out! Does your preferred man have a barking problem when he doesn't get his own way? I will help you conquer this problem and any jealousy he might display when feeling insecure by different training techniques, including one that is sure to become his favorite training tip; touching!

This section provides hands-on training tips that will be pleasurable to execute, and will place you in control of the relationship while creating a deeper and more trusting emotional bond with the man in your life.

"No"

How many times in the past have you wanted to say something to your man when you were unhappy with his behavior, but you kept silent because you didn't want to upset or lose him? One word commands are very critical when setting the rules and boundaries of your relationship from the first meeting. Both men and dogs have a difficult time hearing the word, *No* at first, but will become the most important command to teach your man. Let's say you made reservations to have dinner with him, and that night you're expecting to rendezvous, then his best friend calls with two tickets and he just has to go. At the last minute he asks if he can cancel with you. It's up to you to set the standards. Look firmly into his eyes when he's in one of his selfish moods and sternly tell him: *No!* Let him know that you mean *No* and don't back down regardless of what excuse he's concocted. Consistency is the key to making this command work. It's also important to use this command wisely; otherwise your man won't take you seriously or will just laugh or bark it off.

"Come"

The second most useful command is, *Come*. Men and dogs are similar; they both explore new territories and stray whenever their curiosity gets the best of them. And they respond eagerly and equally to the command *Come* because they think they will be getting affection and attention from you. You must use this command every time you sense your man is losing interest, even if it means keeping him on a short leash outdoors and indoors. Don't get alarmed when walking through the park with your man and suddenly he spots a tight-bodied woman on roller blades in short-shorts. Instead, gently place your arm in his, and whisper in his ear that you have a special lingerie treat back at your place you want to try on for him. Teach your man to relate to the command, *Come*, with pleasure and treats. Don't use it to punish him or he'll take off running the first chance he gets!

"Sit"

Men and dogs have short attention spans and difficulty sitting still for long periods of time. Blame it on their natural instinct to play games and hunt! When your man is constantly sniffing around and driving you crazy with his unending distractions, it's time to use the *Sit* command. Encourage your man to sit by leading him to a chair, couch, park bench, and sit first. Then take his hand and guide him next to you while gently saying the word *Sit*. This training tip is exceptionally useful if you're out with friends and/or family at a restaurant and your husband, boyfriend, or date gets up right in the middle of dinner and disappears. When you finally find him talking to the bartender and watching a sports event, escort him back to the table, and say *Sit*. If he gets up again (which is probable if a sports game is on), continue practicing the *Sit* command until he remains seated long enough for you to praise him, give him a nuzzle, or a kiss on the cheek. This command works well with the *Stay* command; *Sit - Stay*. Eventually he will sit long enough for everyone to finish dinner, including him! The *Sit* tip is also helpful when you drag him to a chick flick, clothes shopping, your cousin's wedding, or the ballet!

"Stay"

When it comes to men and dogs they either *Stay* or stray. It's up to you to show your man that it's more advantageous for him to stay than go. The *Stay* command will prevent your man from running out the front door every time it opens, discourage him from flirting with his office hottie, and make him think twice when other dogs call him out to run with the wolves every night. *Stay* works especially well when coupled with the *No* command. As with all the training tips, consistency from the start will produce positive results. Let's say your man is over for a romantic evening and his cell phone rings. He answers, and gets a last minute invitation to join the wild pack at a club opening. He asks if it would be alright if he leaves and catches up with you later. Not what you intended to happen, right? Tell him firmly *No*, it's not okay. And then affectionately, sweetly, and seductively say, *Stay*. Nine times out of ten, he will rethink his options and decide to hang about with you. If this command doesn't work the first time you say *Stay*, try using his name the second time. For example, *Stay Peter*. You'll have the confirming pleasure of watching him melt while turning off his cell phone!

"Down"

Have you ever had one of those nights where you spend two hours primping, getting dressed to perfection (as close as possible), and just as you're ready to walk out the door, your main squeeze gets in one of his feisty moods and starts to jump all over you? If so, here's the training tip for you! Just say *Down*! This is one of the most difficult commands to teach both men and dogs because they live in the moment and tend to get carried away when wanting to play. The *Down* command will require a great deal of time and patience on your part but the results will be well worth your effort. Another situation where the *Down* command is appropriate is when you're having a cocktail party and your husband, boyfriend or date won't leave your guests alone. He has a potential client cornered, chewing his or her ear off. Walk over, gently pull your beau away and sweetly say, *Down*. Again, this command requires repetition to take effect. Don't be surprised if you have to use the *Down* training tip on your man several times on the same night before it finally sinks in!

"Roll Over"

There's nothing more amusing then watching a dog having a playful time and rolling over on command. The *Roll Over* command is especially useful when you want your man to jump off the couch that's he's been lounging on all day to play with you. He won't mind when you incorporate some recreational tickling, touching, and carousing. Say *Roll Over*, when he keeps you up all night snoring like a bear. Since he subconsciously associates *Roll Over* with fun, he'll instantly move over or go belly up while sleeping. Men and dogs both like affectionate touching and having their bellies rubbed. Most men after a good meal will automatically rub their own stomachs when joyfully satiated!

Trick or Treats

Men and dogs love their treats! Both get elated and excited about a new toy, refuse to share it and tend to destroy it. The trick to bestowing treats is to only reward your man when he's behaving in the most positive ways. Treat him when he's attentive, not when he's flirting with every Ms. Thing within a ten-mile radius. Indulge him when he's responsible, showing up for engagements that he'd normally bypass if single and not dating you. Ladies, there's a very fine line between giving him a special new toy for the heck of it and giving him a gift when he truly deserves it. Know the difference, otherwise he'll trick you and expect constant special treatment without warrant. Listen, if your man thinks he can easily get what he wants all the time without making an effort, he'll take it and then leave it! Remember, most men are hunters who love the chase. It's up to you to teach him to appreciate romantic candlelit dinners, featuring his favorite wine and dish. Capping the evening by making a sensual move is a treat that he shouldn't take for granted. Let your man prove himself. Teach him to jump through a few hoops (or over several barrels) before he gets the ultimate reward ... you! And guess what? You'll keep him running back for more if he has to work for the prize!

Housebreaking

Roll up your sleeves. You have your job cut out for you when it comes to housebreaking a man. Men and dogs both mark their territory. Dogs refer back to their wild ancestors, claiming their territory by leaving scent marks, and relieving themselves at home or yard. Modern men claim their territory by leaving worn socks, wet towels and dirty clothes on the floor, back of a chair or end of the bed. Neither men nor dogs do dishes, laundry, or put the toilet seat down and both are terrified by the sound of vacuum cleaners. Actually what your man is doing is possessively claiming his right to leader of the pack, king of the jungle, head of the den, and ultimately scaring away any other men who might dare to threaten his domain. When he does leave his clothes and wet towels thrown around your home, tell him *No* immediately. Suggest that he pick up after himself right away, leaving less of a mess for later. Don't rub his nose in it, instead pet and praise him when he does clean up after himself without prompting. Create routines when it comes to housebreaking your main squeeze, no matter how much he barks and whines about it.

We've all heard the saying; *You can't teach an old dog new tricks!* Take a deep breath and call on your strength, if you're marrying a confirmed bachelor, living with a man whose previous girlfriend let him get away with murder, or newly cohabiting with a mama's boy. You'll have to create and enforce house rules more rigorously than you would with a puppy. Your saving grace is that men and dogs like to have a designated space they can claim as their own. Take the initiative and create a special room for him, whether it be a den, work room, game room, or any place that he can mess up as often as he would like without putting him in the doghouse! The irony of it all is that this is the one room he will probably keep immaculate!

The Leash

Men and dogs are similar; some are easier to keep on a leash while others take a little more patience and perseverance to train. You'll determine the length of the leash right from the beginning of your relationship. Start by keeping your man on a tight leash, close to your side, until he learns to walk beside you -- not in front of or behind you. Here is the trick for when you're not with him: ease up on the grip and he'll find himself missing the tight hold. When you're apart, give him more rope (hopefully he won't choke himself), and it will build trust between the two of you. You know the time is right to let the leash out a little when you're on the beach, and he only has eyes for your legs, while rubbing suntan lotion all over you! Ladies, remember: men will always be dogs, so you can never take them off the leash completely!

Jealousy

The green-eyed monster strikes both men and dogs alike! Men's emotions are obviously more complex than dogs. The comparison is jealousy emerges when both feel insecure, threatened and have to compete for more attention. The training tip here is to tame your man's aroused jealousy by reassuring him and offering an extra expression of affection. An unexpected kiss, hug, night on the town, or tickets to his favorite sporting event will make him feel special and appreciated. If an ex shows up at a social setting and starts talking to you about the good old days, and your present steady date starts to shows signs of jealousy, don't discuss it until you get home. Don't put him on the spot or he might feel more territorially threatened and start a dogfight! You'll have more success calming your man when the object of his competition isn't around. Jealousy can cause aggressiveness. Encourage your main squeeze to exercise daily at the gym or participate in healthy physical activity to positively channel misplaced anger. If he's more confident, he'll conquer feelings of inadequacy, keep jealousy at bay, and hold you closer.

Touching

Petting men and dogs is equally important because it encourages pleasurable affectionate responses from both. Touching, massaging, running your hands through your man's hair, playfully scratching his back, and nurturing, will strengthen the bond between you and make him feel happy and secure. If the man in your life has been hurt or mistreated in a past relationship, constant reassurance and touching will mend his heartbreak and heal old wounds. Touching will promote trust within your relationship. When your man experiences trust with you, he will carry it to the outside world, thinking it's not such a scary place out there! He'll benefit socially and professionally from having this loving, affectionate connection with you. Don't forget if he's financially successful that means he'll bring home a bone or two to share with you. Off you go to the hairdresser, health spa or boutique for an overall grooming session!

Problem Barking

The two primary reasons that men and dogs bark, howl, and whine, originates from normal insecurity and separation anxiety. Have you noticed that a man will have a bone to pick with you, when you're going on a girl's night out, business trip, or visiting family and friends without him? However annoying, it's his very unique way of telling you he doesn't want you to leave. When he starts barking unreasonably, use the *No* command. Then secure him by touching, giving him a hug, a kiss, or an affectionate gesture. Make it perfectly clear that he has absolutely nothing to worry about. You will return! If your husband or boyfriend begins to whine when you ask him to participate in house chores, reassure him that the vacuum won't hurt him!

Chapter 4

Success Tails

*A dog is one of the remaining reasons why some people
can be persuaded to go for a walk.*

O. A. Battista

WHAT'S A BOOK ABOUT DATING, romance, love, and marriage without a few happy endings? This chapter provides true success stories that are doggone funny ... and will reveal the positive effects that dogs can have on your life. I'll reveal how dogs have altered the fates of different people and situations, teaching us that we should never downplay the importance of our cute canines, who were destined to be in our lives. The heartwarming stories will surely make you bark out loud when you read about the antics and love inspiration the dogs offered! Men planning to propose to their girlfriends are always looking for unique and clever ways to do it. I'll share with you some of the most doggone-friendly marriage proposals and one that went awry but turned into happy endings at the last fateful moment. These success stories will not only entertain you, but will provide the man in your life with some creative new ideas on how he can include his dog when he decides to pop the question, plan a special anniversary celebration, or present you with a unique holiday gift. Curious? Read on!

Heather & Frank

Frank and his girlfriend, Heather, dated for about five years when he finally got up the nerve to ask for her hand in marriage. They knew for years that they wanted a dog and Frank thought this would be the perfect opportunity to combine two fabulous life-altering choices. He discovered that miniature Schnauzers tickled Heather's fancy. Schnauzers are loving, devoted, protective, enthusiastic, and patient with children. Frank set off to find a responsible breeder. He did his research and found a breeder in upstate New York. The Schnauzer puppies would be ready for a new home in about a month, which gave Frank time to purchase the engagement ring and put his plan in motion.

On the sly, Frank went upstate and chose the most adorable puppy in the litter. He gave the breeder a special tag and collar to be worn by the puppy on the day he scheduled to pick up the furry bundle of joy. Frank's plan was gaining momentum!

A month later Frank and Heather drove upstate for what she thought was a casual ride through the country. Frank purchased a beautiful engagement ring for Heather and kept the puppy a secret surprise for her. They passed the breeder's house that had a sign out front reading "Puppies for Sale". Frank insisted they pull over. The breeder brought the puppy out and handed it to Heather. She could hardly hide her excitement when she saw the miniature Schnauzer pup. She read the tag around his neck, *HEATHER, WILL YOU MARRY ME?* After a moment of confusion, Frank was on one knee, Heather was crying, and the pup was licking her face. Heather later remarked, "Having Junior participate in my engagement to Frank was the most memorable moment of my life!"

Pam & Larry

Pam & Larry's success story had many twists and turns before their story was a complete success! Larry wished his proposal went as smoothly as Frank's. Larry had the original idea of using his Yorkshire Terrier, Hank, to pop the question to his girlfriend Pam. Yorkies are spunky stubborn dogs who like to be in the center of all activities. In anticipation of her homecoming from a successful business trip, Larry tied the wedding ring within a thin white ribbon around Hank's neck. Pam called Larry to let him know she would be a little late arriving home. When Larry turned around to take the ring from around the dog's neck, the ring and the ribbon were gone! Larry frantically searched the apartment, coming to the realization that Hank must have chewed through the ribbon and swallowed the ring. He quickly put Hank in the car and just as he was about to pull out of the driveway, Pam returned home. When she asked Larry what happened, he told her that Hank swallowed some aspirin and he was taking him to have his stomach pumped. He didn't want to give away the fact that he was getting ready to propose to her and Hank had swallowed the ring.

A concerned Pam jumped into the car and they were off to the hospital. At the hospital, Larry insisted on speaking with the doctor alone, claiming Pam was too hysterical. The doctor took X-rays and located the ring right smack in the middle of Hank's stomach. Larry sighed with relief when the doctor assured him the dog would be fine. A worried Pam was led into the examining room. With the X-ray lit up on the screen, Larry pointed out the ring in Hank's stomach. Larry then got down on one knee and proposed to Pam. Pam was thrilled and told Larry she was sure the ring was beautiful and couldn't wait to have it out of Hank's stomach and on her finger. Pam, Larry and Hank lived happily ever after.

Stephanie & Glenn

Stephanie and Glenn dated for seven years when Glenn decided the time was right to make it official. Glenn knew he wanted their Golden Retriever, Caesar, to be an integral part of their engagement. Golden Retrievers are smart dogs and can be trained easily. Caesar, being a creature of habit, always buried the same bone in the same spot in their backyard. This gave Glenn a brilliant idea! He searched in antique shops and flea markets for an antique wooden box until he found just the one he was looking for. Glenn engraved, *I LOVE YOU SWEETHEART - WILL YOU MARRY ME?* on the outside of the antique box. He quickly buried the box with the engagement ring and secured Caesar's favorite bone inside. Right on time, Caesar began to dig. Glenn anxiously called to Stephanie to come quickly, that Caesar had dug up something very interesting.

Stephanie and Glenn stood over Caesar digging and scratching at the box. Stephanie bent down to see what it was. Glenn told her to pick it up and see what was inside. Stephanie was mortified and said it was probably the coffin of someone's dead hamster. Glenn picked up the box, rubbed the dirt off the top and read the engraving out loud to Stephanie. She wondered whose it was and how long it had been there. When Stephanie opened the box and saw Caesar's bone and a beautiful diamond and sapphire wedding ring, she laughed and then she cried. "It was so within Glenn's character to propose engagement using Caesar in a funny and touching way," Stephanie laughed. Stephanie and Glenn saved Caesar's favorite bone for posterity. Caesar ran off with the box, and it didn't fare as well!

Chapter 5

A List of Places to Rescue Your Perfect Dog

THE FOLLOWING IS A DIRECTORY of credible and well-established animal organizations throughout the United States and Puerto Rico. The locations and contact information will aid in your search for a new canine companion. You should have a keener sense of what dog best suits you after reading the characteristics and personalities of each breed. Whether you're looking for a playful, entertaining pup; a loyal, protective pooch; or a perfect family dog, by contacting these organizations you will be sure to find the dog of your dreams. Good luck, and have fun in your quest for that lucky dog!

ALL U.S.

Humane Community of America
P.O. Box 450715
Atlanta, GA 31145
770-220-0603
www.saveourstrays.com

www.petfinder.com
Search for pets or shelters
throughout U.S. by city and state

ALABAMA

The Greater Birmingham Humane Society
1713 Lomb Ave.
Birmingham, AL 35208
205-780-7281
www.gbhs.org

Humane Society of Etowah County
1700 Chestnut St.
Gadsden, AL 35901
256-547-4846
microxl.com/hsociety

ALASKA

Alaska SPCA
7309 Arctic Blvd.
Anchorage, AK 99518
907-344-3622
www.alaskaspca.org

The Gastineau Humane
7705 Glacier Highway
Juneau, Alaska 99801
907-789-0260
www.ghspets.org

ARIZONA

Arizona Humane Society
1521 W. Dobbins Road
Phoenix, AZ 85041
602-997-7586
www.azhumane.org

Humane Society of Southern Arizona
3450 North Kelvin Blvd.
Tucson, Arizona 85716
www.humane-so-arizona.org
520-321-3704

ARKANSAS

Humane Society of Palaski County
(Warm Hearts for Cold Noses)
14600 Colonel Glenn Rd.
Little Rock, AR 72210
501-227-6166
www.warmhearts.org

Northeast Arkansas Humane Society
807 Strawfloor Rd.
Jonesboro, AR 72401
870-932-5185
www.neahs.org

CALIFORNIA

The Amanda Foundation
351 Foothill Rd.
Beverly Hills, CA 90210
310-278-2935
www.amanda-fnd.org

Los Angeles SPCA
5026 W Jefferson Blvd.
Los Angeles, CA 90016
www.spcala.com

Much Love Animal Rescue
P.O. Box 341721
Los Angeles, CA 90034-1721
310-636-9115
www.muchlove.org

San Diego Humane Society and SPCA
5500 Gaines St.
San Diego, CA 92110
619-299-7012
www.sdhumane.org

Peninsula Humane Society and SPCA
12 Airport Blvd.
San Marco, CA 94401
650-340-7022
www.peninsulahumanesociety.org

COLORADO

Colorado Humane Society & SPCA
2760 S. Platte River Dr.
Englewood, CO 80110
303-781-9344
www.coloradohumane.org

Humane Society of Denver
Denver Dumb Friends League
2080 South Quebec St.
Denver, CO 80231
303-751-5772
www.ddfl.org

CONNECTICUT

The Connecticut Humane Society
701 Russell Rd.
Newington, CT 06111
860-594-4500
www.cthumane.org

The Connecticut Humane Society
The Bethany Shelter
788 Amity Road (Route 63)
Bethany, CT 06524-3016
203-393-0150
www.cthumane.org

The Connecticut Humane Society
The Waterford Shelter
169 Old Colchester Road
Quaker Hill, CT 06375-0041
860-442-8583
www.cthumane.org

The Connecticut Humane Society
The Westport Shelter
455 Post Road East
Westport, CT 06880-4435
203-227-4137
www.cthumane.org

DELAWARE

Delaware SPCA
Newcastle County Shelter
455 Stanton Christiana Rd.
Newark, DE 19713
302-998-2281
www.delspca.org

FLORIDA

Humane Society of Greater Miami
North Shelter
2101 N.W. 95th St.
Miami, FL 33147
305-696-0800
www.humanesocietymiami.org

Humane Society of Greater Miami
South Shelter
16601 S.W. 117th Ave.
Miami, Florida 33177
305-252-3389
www.humanesocietymiami.org

Jacksonville Humane Society
8464 Beach Boulevard
Jacksonville, FL 32216
904-725-8766
www.jaxhumane.org

SPCA of Central Florida
Orange County Shelter
2727 Conroy Rd.
Olrando, FL 32839
407-351-7722
www.ohs-spca.org

SPCA of Central Florida
Seminole County Shelter
2800 County Home Rd.
Sanford, FL 32773
407-323-8685
www.ohs-spca.org

GEORGIA

Atlanta Humane Society and SPCA
981 Howell Mill Rd. NW
Atlanta, GA 30318-5562
404-875-5331
www.atlhumane.org

Humane Society Chatham/Savannah
7515 Salle Mood Dr.
Savannah, GA 31406
912-354-9515
www.savannah-humane.com

HAWAII

Hawaiian Humane Society
2700 Waialae Ave.
Honolulu, HI 96826
808-946-2187
www.hawaiianhumane.org

Maui Humane Society
P.O. Box 1047
Puunene, HI 96784
808-877-3680
www.mauihumane.org

IDAHO

Bannock County Humane Society
P.O. Box 332
850 Barton Rd.
Pocatello, ID 83204
208-232-0371
www.bannockhumanesociety.org

Idaho Humane Society
4775 W. Doorman St.
Boise, ID 83705
208-342-3508
www.idahohumanesociety.com

ILLINOIS

The Anti-Cruelty Society
510 N. LaSalle
Chicago, IL 60610
312-644-8338
www.anticruelty.org

Humane Society of Central Illinois
Pet Adoption Center
3001 Gill St.
Bloomington, IL 61704-9638
309-664-7387
www.hscipets.org

Paws Chicago
1110 W 35th St.
Chicago, IL 60609
773-935-PAWS
www.pawschicago.org

Red Door Animal Shelter
P.O. Box 269119
Chicago, IL 60626
773-764-2242
www.reddoorshelter.org

INDIANA

Humane Society of Indianapolis
7929 North Michigan Rd.
Indianapolis, IN 46268
317-872-5650
www.indyhumane.com

The Humane Society of Jackson County
P.O. Box 135
1109 G Avenue West, Freeman Field
Seymour, IN 47274
812-522-5200
www.jchumane.org

KANSAS

The Humane Society of
Greater Kansas City
5445 Parallel Pkwy.
Kansas City, KS 66104
913-596-1000
www.hsgkc.org

Helping Hands Humane Society, Inc.
2625 NW Rochester Rd.
Topeka, KS 66617-1201
785-233-7325
www.topekahumaneshelter.og

KENTUCKY

Kentucky Humane Society
"Lifelong Friends"
241 Steedly Dr.
Louisville, KY 40214
502-366-3355
www.kyhumane.org

Woodford Humane Society
890 Tyrone Pike (Animal Shelter Road)
P.O. Box 44
Versailles, KY 40383
859-873-5491
www.woodfordhumanesociety.org

LOUISIANA

Iberia Humane Society "Have a Heart"
P.O. Box 11422
New Iberia, LA 70562-1422
337-365-1923
www.iberiahumane.com

New Orleans SPCA
1319 Japonica St.
New Orleans, LA 70117
504-944-7445
www.la-spca.org

St. Tammany Humane Society
20384 Harrison Ave.
Covington, LA 70433
985-893-9474
www.sthsonline.net

MAINE

Greater Androscoggin Humane Society
3312 Hotel Rd.
Auburn, ME 04210
207-783-2311
www.gahumane.org

Humane Society of Knox County
P.O. Box 1294
Rockland, ME 04841
207-594-2200
www.humanesocietyofknoxcounty.org

MARYLAND

Fredrick County Humane Society
5712 D Industry Ln.
Frederick, MD 21704
301-694-8300
www.fchs.org

The Maryland SPCA
3300 Falls Road
Baltimore, MD 21211
410-235-8826
www.mdspca.org

MASSACHUSETTS

Animal Rescue League of Boston
P.O. Box 265
Boston, MA 02116
617-426-9170
www.arl-boston.org

Massachusetts SPCA
350 South Huntington Ave.
Boston, MA 02130
617-522-7400
www.mspca.org

Northeast Animal Shelter
P.O. Box 4506
Salem, MA 01970-0901
978-745-9888
www.northeastanimalshelter.org

MICHIGAN

Michigan Humane Society (Main Office)
26711 Northeastern Hwy., Suite 175
Southfield, MI 48034
248-799-7400
www.mihumane.org

Michigan Humane Society (Detroit)
7401 Chrysler Dr.
Detriot, MI 48211
313-872-3400
www.mihumane.org

Michigan Humane Society
(Rochester Hills)
3600 Auburn Rd.
Rochester Hills, MI 48309
248-852-7420
www.mihumane.org

Michigan Humane Society (Westland)
37255 Marquette
Westland, MI 48185
734-721-7300
www.mihumane.org

MINNESOTA

Humane Society for Companion Animals
1115 Beulah Ln.
St. Paul, MN 55108
651-645-7387
www.hsca.net

Humane Society for Companion Animals
9785 Hudson Rd.
Woodbury, MN 55125
651-730-6008
www.hsca.net

Northwoods Humane Society
Forest Lake, MN 55025
651-982-0240
www.northwoodshs.org

MISSISSIPPI

Humane Society of South Mississippi
13756 Washington Ave.
Gulfport, MS 39507
228-863-3354
www.hssm.org

Pearl River County SPCA
P.O. Box 191
Picayune, MS 39466
601-798-8000
www.prcspca.org

MISSOURI

Animal Protection Agency
1705 S. Hanley Rd.
Brentwood, MO 63144-2909
314-645-4610
www.apamo.org

Humane Society of Missouri
St. Louis Adoption Center
1201 Macklind Ave.
St. Louis, MO 63110
314-951-1562
www.hsmo.org

MONTANA

Humane Society of Gallatin Valley
2125 N. Rouse
Bozeman, MT 59715
406-587-0456
www.montanapets.org

Rimrock Humane Society
P.O. Box 834
Roundup, MT 59072
406-323-3687
www.rimrockhumanesociety.org

NEBRASKA

Central Nebraska Humane Society
1312 Sky Park Rd.
Grand Island, NE 68801
308-385-5305
www.tails.petfinder.com

Nebraska Humane Society
8929 Fort St.
Omaha, NE 68134-2899
402-444-7800
www.nehumanesociety.org

NEVADA

Nevada Humane Society
200 Kresge Ln.
Sparks, NV 89431
775-331-5770
www.nevadahumanesociety.org

Las Vegas Valley Humane Society
PMB438
2250 East Tropicana Rd., Suite 19
Las Vegas, NV 89119
702-434-2009
www.lvvhumane.org

NEW HAMPSHIRE

Humane Society for Greater Nashua
24 Ferry Rd.
Nashua, NH 03064-8109
603-889-BARK
www.hsfn.org

New Hampshire Humane Society
P.O. Box 572
1305 Meredith Center Rd.
Laconia, NH 03246
603-524-3252
www.nhhumane.org

New Hampshire SPCA
104 Portsmouth Ave.
Stratham, NH 03885
603-772-2921
www.nhspca.org

NEW JERSEY

Animal Rescue Force
P.O. Box 418
East Brunswick, NJ 08816
732-257-7559
www.petfinder.org/shelters/NJ16.html

Mt. Pleasant Animal Shelter
194 Route 10 West
East Hanover, NJ 07936
973-386-0590
www.njshelter.org

NEW MEXICO

Heart and Soul Animal Sanctuary
369 Montezuma Ave., Suite 130
Sante Fe, N.M. 87501
505-757-6817
www.animal-sanctuary.org

Humane Society of Taos, Inc.
P.O. Box 622
1200 St. Francis Ln.
Toas, N.M. 87571
505-758-9708
www.taoshumane.com

NEW YORK

Animal Rescue Fund of the Hamptons
Daniel's Hole Rd.
P.O. Box 901
Wainscott, NY 11975
631-537-0400
www.arfhamptons.org

ASPCA
424 East 92nd St.
New York, NY 10128-6804
212-876-7700
www.aspca.org

Central New York SPCA
5878 East Molloy Rd.
Syracuse, NY 13211
315-454-4479
www.cnyspca.org

Green Chimneys Children's Services
and Green Chimneys School
(human/animal interactions)
400 Doansburg Rd., Caller Box 719
Brewster, NY 10509-0719
845-279-2995
www.greenchimneys.org

Humane Society of New York
306 East 59th St.
New York, NY 10022
212-752-4842
www.humanesocietyny.org

SPCA of Westchester
590 North State Rd.
Briarcliff Manor, NY 10510
914-941-2894
www.spca914.com

Stray from the Heart
P.O. Box 11
New York, NY 10024-0011
212-726-DOGS
www.strayfromtheheart.org

Suffolk County SPCA
363 Route 111
Smithtown, NY 11787
631-382-SPCA
www.suffolkspca.org

NORTH CAROLINA

Humane Society of Charlotte
2700 Toomey Avenue
Charlotte, NC 28203
704-377-0534
www.clthumane.org

SPCA of Cumberland County
3232 Bragg Blvd.
Fayetteville, NC 28303
910-860-1177
www.spcaofcumberlandco.bizland.com

NORTH DAKOTA

The Natural Pet Center
1345 South University Dr.
Fargo, ND 58103
701-239-0110

Pet Connection Humane Society
730 Highway 804 NE
Bismarck, ND 58503
701-222-2719
www.petcon.org

OHIO

Geauga Humane Society
15463 Chillicothe
Russell Township, OH 44072
440-338-4819
www.geaugahumane.org

Capital Area Humane Society
(Central Ohio)
3015 Scioto-Darby Executive Court
Hillard, OH 43026
614-777-PETS
www.cahs-pets.org

Humane Society of Allen County
3606 Elida Road
Lima, OH 45807
419-991-1775
www.hsoac.org

OKLAHOMA

Humane Society of Stillwater
1710 S. Main St.
Stillwater, OK 74074
405-377-1701
www.hspets.org

Pets and People Humane Society
701 Inla
Yukon, OK 73085
405-350-PETS
www.petsandpeople.com

OREGON

Oregon Humane Society
1067 NE Columbia Blvd.
Portland, OR 97211
503-285-7722
www.oregonhumane.org

Humane Society of Central Oregon
61170 S.E. 27th Street
Bend, OR 97702
541-382-3537
www.hsco.org

PENNSYLVANIA

Pennsylvania SPCA
350 E. Erie Ave.
Philadelphia, PA 19134
215-426-6300
www.pspca.org

PUERTO RICO

Save a Sato foundation
Villas de Cappara, D-2 Calle C
Guaynabo, Puerto Rico 00966
www.saveasoto.org

RHODE ISLAND

Providence Animal Rescue League
34 Elbow Street
Providene, RI 02903
401-421-1399
www.parl.org

Animal Rescue League of Southern
Rhode Island
P.O. Box 458
Wakefield, RI 02880-0458
401-783-7606
www.southkingstown.com

SOUTH CAROLINA

John Ancrum SPCA
3861 Leeds Avenue
Charleston, SC 29405
843-747-4849
www.jaspca.com

Oconee County Humane Society
321 Camp Road
Walhalla, SC 29691-4811
864-638-8798
www.oconeehumanesociety.org

SOUTH DAKOTA

Aberdeen Area Humane Society
13452 385th Ave.
Aberdeen, SD 57401-8400
605-226-1200
www.anewleashonlife.net

Sioux Falls Area Humane Society
3720 East Benson Road
Sioux Falls, SD 57104
605-338-4441
www.sfhumanesociety.com

TENNESSEE

Humane Society of Clarksville-
Montgomery County
P.O. Box 571
Clarksville, TN 37401
931-648-8042
www.clarksvillehumansociety.org

The Humane Society of
the Tennessee Valley
800 Millwood Road Po Box 9479
Knoxville, TN 37940
865-573-9675
www.humanesocietytennessee.com

TEXAS

The Humane Society & SPCA -Austin
124 W. Anderson Lane
Austin, TX 78752
512-837-7985
www.austinspca.com

Houston SPCA
900 Portway Dr.
Houston, TX 77024
713-869-SPCA
www.spcahouston.org

SPCA of Texas
362 S. Industrial Blvd
Dallas, TX 75207
1-888-ANIMALS
214-651-9611
www.spca.org

UTAH

CAWS Community Animal
Welfare Society
P.O. Box 17825
Salt Lake City, UT 84117
801-328-4731
www.caws.org

Best Friends Animal Sanctuary
5001 Angel Canyon Rd.
Kanab, UT 84741-5001
435-644-2001
www.bestfriends.org/index.htm

VERMONT

Addison County Humane Society
236 Boardman Street
Middlebury, VT 05753
802-388-1100
staff@addisonhumane.org

Frontier Animal Society of Vermont
502 Strawberry Acres Rd
Newport, VT 05855
802-754-2228
www.frontieranimalsociety.org

VIRGINIA

Virginia Beach SPCA
3040 Holland Road
Virginia Beach, VA 23456
757-427-0070
www.vbspca.com

Richmond SPCA
2519 Hermitage Road
Richmond, VA 23220
804-643-6785
www.richmondspca.org

WASHINGTON

Seattle Animal Shelter
2061 15th Ave.
West Seattle, WA 98119
206-386-PETS
www.seattleanimalshelter.org

The Humane Society for Seattle
King County
13212 SE Eastgate Way
Bellevue, Washington 98005-4408
425-641-0080
www.seattlehumane.org

Humane Society for
Southwest Washington
2121 St. Francis Lane
Vancouver, WA 98660
360-693-4746
www.sw-wa-humanesociety.org

WASHINGTON D.C.

The Washington Animal Rescue League
71 Oglethorpe St., NW
Washington, D.C. 20011
202-726-2556
www.warl.org

Washington Humane Society
7319 Georgia Ave., NW
Washington, D.C. 20012
202-576-6664
www.washhumane.org

District of Columbia Animal Shelter
(Run by Washington Humane Society)
1201 New York Ave, NE
Washington, D.C. 20002
202-576-6664
www.washhumane.org

WEST VIRGINIA

Berkeley County Humane Society
554 Charles Town Rd
Martinsburg, WV 25401
304-267-8389
Berkeley.wvhumane.com

Kanawha/Charleston Humane Society
1248 Greenbrier St.
Charleston, WV 25311
304-342-1576
www.wvanimalshelter.com

WISCONSIN

The Chippewa County Humane
Association
10503 CTH S South
Chippewa Falls, WI 54729
715-382-4832

Forest County Humane Society
701 Industrial Way
Crandon, WI 54520
715-478-2098
www.chippewahumane.org

EVERY DOG NEEDS
A GOOD HOME!

Animal Fair

A Lifestyle Magazine for Animal Lovers

Travel Issue

Jane Clayson
Jeff Corwin
Edie Falco
Doris Roberts

TIME TO TRAVEL
Australia
Sweden
Italy

Washington D.C.
New York
Boston
Maine

CHARLIZE THERON
angel to the animals

www.animalfair.com
$3.99US $4.99CAN

Anim

A Lifestyle Magazine for Anim

Pads For Pets

Feng Shui
Design

Designing the
Perfect Dog

Pet Friendly
Apartments

www.animalfair.com
$3.99US $5.99CAN

Winona

Fair

Design Issue

HANIA
TWAIN

Sings Pet Praises

Arnold • Ali Wentworth
Lola Osbourne

Animal Fair

A Lifestyle Magazine for Animal Lovers and Pet Owners
PREMIERE 1999

and their famous people

Mira Sorvino
Brad Pitt
Wendy Wasserstein
Ross Bleckner
Mariah Carey
Tom Hanks

Renee Zellweger

Silver Screen Star and Her Top Dog

Your Own
Private Africa

Designers Dress Dogs
Fashion Unleashed!

Saving Private Lion
Inside!

www.animalfair.com

Animal Fair

ABOUT THE AUTHOR

WENDY DIAMOND is founder and editorial director of Animal Fair (fairness to animals), a lifestyle magazine for pet owners. Her other accomplishments include two bestselling cookbooks, *A Musical Feast* and *An All-Star Feast*, featuring recipes donated by celebrities and athletes that benefited charities. She's the leading authority on animal lifestyles, and in 2002, she starred in the critically acclaimed TV show, *Single in the City*, where she and Lucky went off in search of Mr. Right (Breed). She hosts a weekly pet segment on CBS New York. Wendy was born in Chagrin Falls, Ohio and currently lives in New York with Pasha, her rescued Russian Blue cat, and Lucky, her six-pound Maltese. She's still searching for that lucky Mr. Right. For more information, please visit: www.animalfair.com.